SHANE MARQUIN VAN ROOYEN

Angels In Human Form Does Exist on Earth

If you ever doubt about angels in your life read this and know the angels in your life

Contents

Foreword

Introduction

This compelling book delves into the extraordinary reality of angels existing all around us, drawing upon the author's own profound personal experiences. Challenging the skepticism that often surrounds the concept of angelic beings, the author provides a captivating firsthand account of a remarkable encounter that sheds light on the very real presence of these celestial guardians in our midst. Through this enlightening written work, readers are invited to embark on a transformative journey of spiritual discovery, exploring the subtle yet powerful ways in which angels make their influence known in our day-to-day lives. With vulnerable honesty and keen insight, the author guides us in learning to recognize the telltale signs of angelic intervention, dispelling doubts and empowering us to fully acknowledge the divine assistance available to us all.

Far more than just an abstract theological discussion, this book offers a profoundly personal exploration of the mystical realm, providing a roadmap for tuning into the subtle energies and synchronicities that point to the angels actively supporting and guiding us, if only we open our eyes to perceive them. Prepare to have your eyes opened to the extraordinary reality unfolding all around you, as you discover the angels that have been with you all along, waiting to be recognized and welcomed into your life.

Angels are truly remarkable heavenly beings, sent by the divine hand of God himself to watch over and guide humanity. These celestial entities are the most powerful and exalted of all of God's creations, possessing immense strength, wisdom, and supernatural abilities that far surpass the comprehension of mortal men. Angels are tasked with a wide range of responsibilities, from shielding the faithful from harm to intervening in the affairs of the world to fulfill the will of God Almighty.

What makes angels all the more wondrous is their ability to take on human form when the situation demands it. Rather than appearing in their full, awe-inspiring glory, angels will sometimes choose to manifest as ordinary people, blending seamlessly into the tapestry of human society. This shapeshifting capability allows them to move freely among us, carrying out their divine missions in ways that are subtle and unobtrusive. Whether appearing as radiant, winged guardians or as humble, inconspicuous strangers, angels are always working tirelessly to provide protection, offer guidance, and do the bidding of the Lord. Their power is a gift from on high, a tangible expression of God's love and concern for His children on Earth. Though we may not always be aware of their presence, angels walk among us every day, serving as conduits of divine grace and mercy, and reminding us that we are never truly alone in this world.

The concept of angels existing in human form is a fascinating and captivating notion that has captured the imagination of people throughout history.

These divine beings, often depicted with ethereal wings and glowing halos, are traditionally thought to exist in a realm beyond our physical world. However, the idea that they may walk among us, taking on the appearance of ordinary individuals, imbues the world around us with a sense of mystery and the potential for the extraordinary.

Ponder, for a moment, the possibility that you may have crossed paths with an angel without even realizing it - perhaps that kind stranger who offered assistance in your time of need, or the wise mentor who imparted invaluable guidance. These celestial entities, in their infinite compassion, may choose to cloak themselves in human guise, their true nature hidden from mortal eyes, in order to better serve and uplift humanity. Imagine the wonder of such an encounter, to be graced by the presence of a being of pure light and love, masquerading as a fellow traveler on life's journey. This book invites you to open your heart and mind to the prospect of angels in our midst, reminding us that the divine may manifest in the most unexpected of ways, if only we have the eyes to see and the faith to believe.

* * *

Acknowledgement

Thanks to those who sees this work valuable, those who buy and read, those who share what they have read. Thanks to those readers who want to know more from God. He is our light and our salvation. I acknowledge draft2digital/ Reedsy.com/Amazon/Smashwords and all distribution who make this work available. ALL bookstores online and offline, all libraries all around the world. My work I available to all who seek God's face above anything else. Acknowledging the Church of Christ in general, for the assistance for the work of God to spread the Good news, The Open Door Evangelism & Outreach Ministry S.A for guidance and trust in my work.

Thank you all and may God continues to prosper you.

Chapter 1

CHAPTER 1

Understanding the angelic realm

In my previous work, I briefly touched upon the profound and transformative experiences I have had of encountering God and His angels on a personal level at various points throughout my life.

However, I acknowledge that I did not delve deeply enough into fully explaining the connection and significance of these divine encounters.

These types of mystical, spiritual experiences are truly rare and life-changing for those who are blessed to have them.

When one is graced with a direct interaction with the divine, it can shake the very foundations of their understanding of the world and their place within it.

The veil between the physical and spiritual realms parts, allowing an individual a glimpse into the ineffable mysteries of the universe and the loving, guiding presence of the Almighty. These moments of sacred communion often leave an indelible mark, instilling a sense of awe, humility, and a deep, unwavering faith that transcends the material constraints of everyday existence.

The insights gleaned and the transformative impact of these supernatural encounters are truly difficult to put into words, as they operate on a plane beyond the limitations of human language. Yet, my willingness to share these profoundly personal experiences has the power to inspire and uplift others, offering a tantalizing window into the wondrous possibilities that lie beyond the confines of our mortal understanding.

By delving deeper into the intricate, multifaceted nature of my divine connections, I have the opportunity to guide others on a journey of spiritual awakening and renewal.

To truly understand the nature of life and the mechanisms that govern its workings, one must first seek to comprehend the divine, omnipotent force that lies at the very foundation of existence itself , who is God.

The Almighty God who created all of universe, though inherently spiritual in essence, holds dominion over all realms, both physical and metaphysical.

It is through God's sovereign will and infinite power that the seemingly impossible is manifested into tangible reality, even upon the earthly plane.

Every facet of the natural world, from the grandest celestial bodies to the most minute microorganisms, owes its very being to the creative genius of the divine.

God's reach extends far beyond the comprehension of mortal minds, transcending the constraints of time and space to orchestrate the intricate tapestry of life according to a higher purpose.

By aligning our understanding with the nature of God, we unlock the keys to unraveling the profound mysteries that permeate our world. For the divine spark that ignites the flame of existence resides not only in the lofty realms of the spiritual, but also courses through the veins of every living thing, connecting all of creation in a sacred, symbiotic dance.

To study life, then, is to study God; to grasp the workings of the universe is to glimpse the mind of the Creator.

It is only by embracing this fundamental truth that we can truly begin to fathom the depth and complexity of the world around us, and our place within it.

Before the world as we know it even came into being, everything that would eventually exist already had a place in the divine realm of God. In the infinite expanse of His eternal consciousness, the blueprints for all of creation were fully formed, awaiting the moment when He would speak them into physical reality.

When God then chose to call forth the heavens and the earth, the stars and the seas, the plants and the animals , all of it sprang into existence according to His perfect plan.

And as each new element of the universe materialized, the Lord looked upon His handiwork and declared it "good"

A testament to the flawless vision He had maintained from the very beginning. For God does not create blindly or haphazardly, but with a clear intent and purpose that extends far beyond our mortal understanding. Every inch of this world, from the grandest galaxy to the most microscopic organism, was meticulously designed by the Creator's own hand and a suoer natural word ,He spoken uoon existence, imbued with His seal of approval before it ever took shape in the physical plane.

In this way, the world we inhabit is not merely a random assortment of matter, but a manifestation of the divine blueprint that has existed within God's eternal consciousness since before time itself began.

All of creation, then, is a reflection of His perfect design, the only testament to His sovereignty, His wisdom, and His incomprehensible power to bring forth that which was previously unseen.

Angels are divine beings that were conceived in the very mind of the Almighty God, crafted with the intention of serving and assisting humanity. Even before the creation of the world, God had already envisioned these ethereal guardians, knowing they would be a force of goodness and light to guide and protect His children on Earth.

Heaven itself has attested to the pure and righteous nature of these celestial entities, for they are imbued with an unwavering commitment to the divine plan and an unshakable devotion to the will of the Creator. Angels exist as messengers, protectors, and companions, charged with intervening in the lives of men and women whenever the Heavenly Father deems it necessary. They are ethereal emissaries, beings of radiant energy who walk among us, most of the times unseen by mortal eyes, yet ever-present to offer solace, strength, and wisdom to those who call upon the name of the Lord.

In their very essence, angels represent the benevolence, mercy, and grace of the Almighty, shining beacons of hope in a world often shrouded in darkness.

For the Heavenly Host is the physical manifestation of God's eternal love for His creation, a tangible reminder that even in our darkest moments, we are never truly alone. The angels stand ever-vigilant, ready to guide the faithful and minister to the lost, bearing witness to the profound truth that the goodness of the divine can be made flesh, that the light of Heaven can illuminate the path for all who seek it.

Now that we've explored some ways in which God's understanding extends towards both angels and humans, I'd like to delve deeper and forge a more personal connection with you, the reader.

Allow me to share some of the profound, life-altering encounters I've experienced with angels in my own past life. These are not mere fanciful tales, but rather true testimonies that have left an indelible mark on my spiritual journey.

Picture this , I was going about my daily routine, unaware of the divine forces quietly at work in the unseen realm, when suddenly, a luminous being appeared before me. Its presence radiated a warmth and serenity that was palpable, and in that moment, I felt a profound sense of peace wash over me. As I gazed into its ethereal eyes, I sensed an ancient wisdom and a profound connection to the divine that left me in awe.

This angel, a messenger from the heavens, had come to offer guidance, comfort and reassurance during a particularly challenging time in my life. Through a series of visions and intuitive nudges, this celestial companion gently steered me towards a path of healing and spiritual awakening that I had long been searching for.

In another instance, I found myself in dire need of protection and intervention.

Beset by dark forces and unseen threats, I cried out in desperation, and to my amazement, a squadron of angels materialized, their wings outstretched like shields, shielding me from harm. I felt enveloped in a cocoon of divine light, my fears and anxieties melting away as these celestial guardians surrounded me. It was as if they had been there all along, silently watching over me, waiting to spring into action when I needed them most.

These are but a glimpse of the profound, life-altering encounters I've had with angels , experiences that have forever changed my perspective on the unseen realms and the limitless ways in which the divine communicates with us.

Let me say to you,

it is remarkable how often we find ourselves in precarious situations, teetering on the edge of disaster, only to emerge unscathed. For the longest time, I could never quite comprehend this phenomenon , how was it that I consistently managed to evade the perils that threatened to me?

It wasn't until I experienced a spiritual awakening that the veil was lifted, and I came to understand the deeper spiritual workings at play in my life. You see, there is always a divine orchestration unfolding behind the scenes, orchestrated by the very hands of God and carried out by His legions of angels.

These celestial guardians, though invisible to the naked eye, are always ever-present, shielding us from harm and guiding us through the treacherous waters of existence. It is their unseen interventions, their subtle nudges and divine protections, that time and again snatch us from the jaws of calamity, enabling us to survive situations that by all logical reasoning should have been our undoing.

This awareness, the realization that there are forces far greater than ourselves at work, safeguarding our every step, is a humbling and awe-inspiring revelation. It imbues our lives with a sense of purpose, a deeper understanding that we are not merely adrift in a chaotic universe, but rather cherished children of the Almighty God who love us and gave us a purposefull life , who watched over us unconditionaly by an army of benevolent spiritual beings.

This knowledge instills in us a perfect gratitude, a reverence for the intricate tapestry of the divine plan that is constantly unfolding, even in our most perilous moments.

The concept of divine orchestration speaks to the belief that there is a higher power, a guiding force, that is shaping and directing the course of events in our world and in our lives. It suggests that there is an intricate, unseen blueprint or plan that is being masterfully implemented, with each individual element falling precisely into place according to a grand, design.

Proponents of this idea see the universe as a brilliantly choreographed symphony, with the Almighty serving as the conductor, seamlessly weaving together the varied melodies and harmonies of human experiences, natural phenomena, and universal forces to produce a magnificent, co-hesive whole. Rather than chaos and randomness, divine orchestration implies an underlying order, purpose, and meaning to our existence , that nothing happens by mere chance, but rather, every occurrence, every coincidence, every twist and turn is strategically orchestrated by a divine hand for reasons that may not always be immediately clear to the human mind, but which are part of a greater, more sublime arrangement. This perspective offers solace and reassurance, empowering individuals to find comfort in the notion that their lives are unfolding according to a higher plan, even amidst the seeming disorder and unpredictability of the world around them.

Angels work in a myriad of captivating ways to connect with the human soul and spirit.

Through the senses, they weave their divine influence, speaking to us in the language we can most readily perceive. Visions and imagery dance before our eyes, stirring emotion and wonder , an ethereal glow, a fleeting silhouette, symbols and signs that beckon us to a higher realm. Likewise, the angels communicate through sound, their voices echoing in our minds as thoughts, impressions, or even audible whispers that make the hairs on our necks stand on end.

And it's not just what we see and hear, but what we smell, taste, and feel that bears the imprint of angelic presence. A sudden waft of a sweet, floral aroma, a surge of unexpected energy or a jolt of inspiration, a delicate but powerful sensation that can only be described as "other-worldly"

These are the physical manifestations of the angels' celestial touch. Through this tapestry, they reach into the very depths of our being, caressing our souls and beckoning us to open our hearts to the divine guidance and support that is ever-present, if only we attune ourselves to perceive it.

In this way, the angels bridge the gap between the spiritual and the material, weaving the sacred and the mundane into a beautiful dance that enlivens, uplifts, and transforms the human experience.

Frequency is indeed a crucial element in the connection between angels and humans. These celestial beings operate on a higher vibrational plane, one that is not always easily accessible to mortal souls. However, angels are ever-present, eagerly awaiting opportunities to guide and assist those open to their divine influence. The frequency at which an individual aligns is largely dependent on their level of spiritual development and the specific angelic realm they are attuned to. Those who have cultivated a deep, reverent relationship with the angelic hierarchy will find their frequencies naturally synchronized, allowing for clear, consistent communication.

Conversely, those earlier in their journey may only briefly catch glimpses or fleeting impressions of angelic presence, their frequencies still out of sync. But with dedicated practice of meditation, prayer, and openness to the unseen, one's vibrational frequency can be raised, expanding the bandwidth through which these entities can channel their wisdom, protection, and support. The dance between human and angel is an intricate one, relying on the individual to attune themselves to the appropriate frequency in order to fully receive the blessings and guidance the angels so eagerly wish to impart. It is not a matter of chance, but rather a sacred unfolding that occurs as one progresses along their spiritual path, their frequency rising to meet the angels halfway.

Though we may not always be consciously aware of it, we are constantly surrounded by a spiritual realm that exists beyond the physical world we perceive with our senses. This invisible, dimension is ever-present, intertwined with the reality we inhabit each day. Just as the air we breathe and the energy that animates all life is imperceptible to our naked eyes, there are definitely this unseen forces, energies, and sentient beings that transcend the material plane. They are the elements and the wellspring from which our physical existence emerges, the unmanifest source that gives rise to the manifest.

Every object, every living creature, every thought and experience we have access to through our physical senses originated first in this spiritual realm before materializing into concrete form.

It is a realm of pure potentiality, of divine intelligence and creative power, from which the entire fabric of our observable universe is woven.

Though we may walk through our days unaware, we are never truly alone, for we are continuously enveloped by this invisible, sentient world , a world that imbues all of creation with sacred purpose and meaning, if only we open our hearts and minds to perceive it.

The driven power of faith is a fundamental aspect of the human experience. As beings with the capacity for complex thought and imagination, we possess an incredible ability to manifest our innermost desires and visions.

The very nature of our consciousness grants us access to a realm of endless possibilities, where the stirrings of the mind can give rise to tangible realities.

When a notion takes root within our psyche, it is not merely a fleeting fancy, but rather the precursor to something greater. That thought, that seed of an idea, has been released from the infinite wellspring of the subconscious, gifted to us as a glimpse into the boundless potential that lies dormant within us.

Just as a dream can be summoned into waking life, these mental impressions are imbued with the power to transform into concrete form. It is through the driven force of faith, the steadfast belief that our innermost visions can and will manifest , we unlock the door to actualizing our most profound aspirations.

By nurturing that unwavering conviction, we harness the very essence of human creativity, channeling the abstract into the tangible and bringing to life that which was once confined to the realm of imagination. This is the true magic of the human spirit , an extraordinary capacity to shape our world, one thought, one dream, one act of faith at a time.

With a deeper understanding of the angelic realm, we can now explore the perfect ways in which angels can manifest and influence our lives. These celestial beings like said exist on a higher plane, yet they are intimately connected to the human experience, acting as spiritual guides and protectors.

Angels comes forth in many forms, from the powerful archangels who oversee the grand workings of the universe, to the gentle guardian angels assigned to watch over each individual soul. They communicate with us through subtle signs and synchronicities, nudging us towards our highest purpose. Some people may feel a divine presence or hear the faint whispers of an angel, while others receive clear visions or messages in their dreams.

Angels can also intervene in our lives during times of crisis, providing comfort, strength, and the courage to overcome challenges. They may even orchestrate chance encounters or open up unexpected doors, divinely orchestrating the events of our lives for our greatest good.

When we become attuned to the angelic realm, we start to see the world through a lens of wonder and magic, miracles recognizing the unseen forces that are always working on our behalf.

By inviting angels into our lives and trusting in their guidance, we can live with a perfect sense of support, protection, and divine.

* * *

CHAPTER 2

ngels does exist

Throughout my life,

I have been blessed with numerous encounters with celestial beings, angelic presences that have made their divine influence known to me in significant and life-altering ways.

These sacred interactions have occurred at pivotal moments, guiding me through challenges, providing comfort in times of distress, and illuminating my path forward with a sense of purpose and wonder

.This is just the beginning of many stories of me to come, take off with me on a life changing journey.

One such encounter happened several years ago, when I found myself at a crossroad, unsure of which direction to take.

Like many of us found ourselves in day by day,

I had been wrestling with an important decision, feeling paralyzed by self-doubt and uncertainty. It was then that a figure appeared before me, emanating a gentle, reassuring glow. This angel spoke to me in a voice that resonated within the depths of my soul, imparting wisdom and clarity that had eluded me. In that transformative moment, the fog lifted, and I was filled with a new sense of peace and clarity about the right course of action.

On another occasion, I was going through an immensely difficult personal crisis, feeling overwhelmed by grief and despair. Just when I thought I could no longer carry on, a celestial presence made itself known, wrapping me in a cloak of comfort and unconditional love. I could feel the warmth of its embrace, the gentle caress of its ethereal wings, as it surrounded me with a tangible, healing energy. In that darkest of hours, this angelic visitation provided me the strength and resilience to persevere, guiding me towards a brighter future.

Throughout my life,

I have been blessed with numerous encounters with celestial beings, angelic presences that have made their divine influence known to me in significant and life-altering ways.

These sacred interactions have occurred at pivotal moments, guiding me through challenges, providing comfort in times of distress, and illuminating my path forward with a sense of purpose and wonder.

This is just the beginning of many stories of me to come, come take off with me on a life changing journey.

One such encounter happened several years ago, when I found myself at a crossroad, unsure of which direction to take.

Like many of us found ourselves in day by day,

I had been wrestling with an important decision, feeling paralyzed by self-doubt and uncertainty. It was then that a figure appeared before me, emanating a gentle, reassuring glow. This angel spoke to me in a voice that resonated within the depths of my soul, imparting wisdom and clarity that had eluded me. In that transformative moment, the fog lifted, and I was filled with a new sense of peace and clarity about the right course of action.

On another occasion, I was going through an immensely difficult personal crisis, feeling overwhelmed by grief and despair. Just when I thought I could no longer carry on, a celestial presence made itself known, wrapping me in a cloak of comfort and unconditional love. I could feel the warmth of its embrace, the gentle caress of its ethereal wings, as it surrounded me with a tangible, healing energy. In that darkest of hours, this angelic visitation provided me the strength and resilience to persevere, guiding me towards a brighter tomorrow.

These are just a few of the many sacred encounters I have been blessed to experience throughout my life's journey and am going to write about many of them in this manuscript.

Each time, I have been left in awe of the divine intervention, the manifestation of heavenly guidance that has time and again lifted me up, reassured me, and set me on a path aligned with my highest good.

It is a privilege to have been graced by these heavanly messengers, and I am forever changed by their benevolent presence in my life.

At first I want to talk more about, the concept of angels and their role in the spiritual realm and the natural world where we at , can seem quite perplexing and difficult to wrap one's head around.

After all, these celestial beings exist in a realm beyond our physical senses, operating on a plane of existence that is not easily observed or understood from our limited human perspective.

However, as one delves deeper into the rich theological and mythological traditions surrounding angels, a more nuanced and captivating picture begins to emerge. Angels are often described as radiant,

otherworldly entities that serve as intermediaries between the divine and the mortal, like I said acting as messengers, protectors, and guides for humanity. They are imbued with incredible spiritual powers, from the ability to move between dimensions to wielding dominion over the forces of nature. Yet, they are also depicted as complex, multifaceted figures, exhibiting a wide range of personalities, temperaments, and specialized functions within the heavenly hierarchy. As one contemplates the sheer vastness and mystery of the angelic realm, it becomes clear that these celestial beings operate according to a profound logic and purpose that transcends our earthly understanding. While the full scope of their nature and abilities may forever elude us, exploring the rich tapestry of angelic lore can open up new vistas of spiritual insight and wonder, shedding light on the profound interconnectedness of the mortal and divine realms.

As a child, I experienced a perfect and captivating phenomenon that set me apart from others, I believe ,

In the tranquility of the night, when my eyes drifted shut, a mesmerizing display would unfold before me - a tapestry of numbers, dancing and intertwining in the darkness. This peculiar visual experience was not merely a fleeting dream, but a persistent, almost hypnotic occurrence that left me intrigued and curious about its deeper meaning.

Alongside this numerical reverie, I also encountered a curious physical sensation , a weightlessness, a feather-like lightness that seemed to envelop my very being.

As I moved through the world, this ethereal quality followed me, imbuing my every step with a sense of effortlessness and grace. It was as if the very laws of gravity bent to accommodate my presence, allowing me to navigate through life with a fluidity and ease that others marveled at.

And indeed, marvel they did.

Wherever I went, I found myself the center of attention, with people drawn to my captivating energy and warmth. They sought out my company, delighting in my presence and the positive vibes I seemed to emanate. This special quality, this innate magnetism, set me apart from my peers, making me the object of admiration and wonder in the eyes of those around me

These experiences, so unique and perfect, must have left a lasting impression, shaping my worldview and self-perception in significant ways.

As a student in primary school, I distinctly remember never having to study or do my homework, yet somehow managing to excel and pass every test or exam with ease.

It was as if I had a secret advantage that allowed me to coast through my academic endeavors without putting in the typical effort required of my peers. Looking back, I can't help but wonder if this uncanny success could be attributed to the presence of guardian angels watching over me, as some may believe. Perhaps it was simply a matter of sheer luck or natural talent that propelled me forward, but I can't help but feel that there was a divine intervention at play.

The idea that God had instructed His angels to guide and protect me, granting me an effortless path to academic triumph, is a fascinating one. Even now, I struggle to fully comprehend how I managed to achieve such remarkable results without the usual studious dedication. As I've grown older and gained more life experience, the significance of the potential existence of angels, even in human form, has become increasingly apparent. I am now compelled to share my story, to testify through the lens of my own life experiences, as I believe the truth of angelic intervention is undeniable. The more one delves into the wealth of information surrounding this topic, the more one comes to appreciate the profound impact these celestial beings can have on our earthly lives.

Looking back, I can recall those times when the challenges before me seemed insurmountable, yet I was somehow able to overcome them with remarkable ease. Tasks that appeared daunting and overwhelming to others were, for me, accomplished with little apparent struggle. It was as if an unseen force was guiding my steps, lending me the strength and determination to push through obstacles that might have crushed the spirits of lesser individuals.

In the later years of my life, I've come to recognize that this uncanny ability to conquer the seemingly impossible was no mere coincidence. Rather, it was the direct result of divine intervention and the watchful presence of angelic beings tasked with ensuring the fulfillment of God's purpose for my life. When the Almighty has a plan in store for us, He does not leave us to navigate the challenges alone. Instead, He dispatches His heavenly messengers to walk alongside us, to shield us from harm, and to empower us to achieve what might otherwise be considered unattainable.

I have witnessed this miraculous phenomenon time and time again, marveling at how the most arduous undertakings , whether in my personal life or professional endeavors , have been transformed into effortless triumphs. It is as if the angels themselves have taken hold of the reins, guiding my path and ensuring that the "impossible" becomes not merely possible, but a seamless reality. This unwavering divine support is a testament to the boundless love and care of our Heavenly Father, who sees the true potential within each of us and moves Heaven and Earth to help us fulfill it.

The existence of angels and their ability to interact with the human realm is a profound and fascinating topic that has captivated the minds and hearts of people for centuries. As the scripture reveals, angels possess the remarkable capacity to take on human form, blending seamlessly into our world and walking among us. These celestial beings, often depicted as radiant, otherworldly figures, can manifest in flesh and blood, gracing us with their divine presence and lending their guidance, protection, and wisdom to those who are attuned to their subtle yet powerful influence. Through these transformations, angels become tangible, relatable entities, shattering the perceived barriers between the spiritual and physical realms. The stories of angelic encounters, where these celestial messengers appear in human guise to impart crucial messages, offer profound insights into the interconnectedness of the heavenly and earthly planes.

These accounts, rich with wonder and spiritual significance, invite us to expand our understanding of the unseen forces that shape our lives, reminding us that we are never truly alone, for angels walk among us, ever-vigilant and ready to intervene on our behalf. The ability of angels to assume human form serves as a profound testament to the boundless compassion and care of the divine, as these ethereal beings willingly don the mantle of mortality to better connect with and uplift humanity. Through these remarkable transformations, the veil between the earthly and the eternal is momentarily lifted, allowing us to catch glimpses of the magnificent tapestry of the universe and the intricate ways in which the spiritual and physical worlds intertwine.

In the pages of this book I will share some of my personal experiences with angels and the impact they have had on my life. These encounters are not fictional but real moments that have shaped my beliefs and perspectives. As you read through my journey you will see how these celestial beings have guided and protected me in times of need. I hope that my stories will inspire you to look for the presence of angels in your own life and to trust in the unseen forces that watch over us.

The notion that an angel is sent out to prepare the way for a newborn child is a deeply profound and inspiring belief. It speaks to the idea that there is a divine, celestial presence watching over and guiding each new life that comes into this world. When a child is born, the arrival of this angel is said to be a tangible sign of the sacred and miraculous nature of the event. This celestial emissary is believed to be there to clear the path, to pave the way, for the child's entrance into the physical realm. It is as if the angel is a heavenly usher, ushering in this new soul with reverence and care. And when we look to the story of Jesus, we see this concept manifested even more vividly. Before the savior was born, an angel - the angel Gabriel - was sent to Mary to announce the coming of the Christ child. This divine messenger delivered the profound news, preparing the way for Jesus' arrival and the profound impact his life would have on the world. It is a beautiful parallel that speaks to the profound spiritual significance that is said to accompany each new birth. The idea that an angel is present, watching over and guiding a child into existence, imbues the miracle of life with an almost sacred, otherworldly quality. It is a belief that speaks to the deep, abiding connection between the earthly and the divine, and the ways in which the heavens themselves rejoice at and attend to the arrival of every precious new life.

* * *

CHAPTER 3

We escape many tragedies because. of the angels present in our lives

This is something we have to take to mind endures within our hearts.

From the very moment we enter this world through natural birth ,each of us is blessed with a unique and profound gift, a personal angel, a celestial guardian that has been with us since the very beginning. This divine companion, invisible yet ever-present, is a testament to the profound mysteries and wonders of the universe. They are not mere figments of imagination or religious allegory, but real spiritual entities whose sole purpose is to guide, protect, and nurture us through the ebbs and flows of our earthly existence.

These angels are not random chance occurrences, but a fundamental part of the human experience, woven into the fabric of our being from the instant we take our first breath. They are our constant companions, whispering words of comfort and strength when we falter, lifting us up when we stumble, and providing an unwavering source of love and support throughout our lives. Their presence is a testament to the deep, abiding care of a higher power, a reassurance that we are never truly alone, even in our darkest moments.

These angels are not merely passive observers, but active participants in our lives, guiding our steps, influencing our decisions, and nudging us towards our highest potential. Through subtle signs and synchronicities, they reveal themselves, encouraging us to trust our intuition, to listen to the quiet voice within that speaks of greater truths. And while their form may remain elusive to our physical eyes, their impact is undeniable, shaping the trajectory of our lives in profound and meaningful ways.

So as we navigate the complexities and challenges of this world, let us take solace in the knowledge that we are never truly alone. For within each of us resides a guardian angel, a celestial companion whose unwavering devotion and divine wisdom are the very foundation upon which we can build our lives, secure in the knowledge that we are forever guided, protected, and loved.

Even before the moment of conception, the divine plan for a child's arrival was already in motion. In the timeless realm of the heavens, God had dispatched one of His celestial messengers, an angel, to descend upon the earth and convey a profound message to a young woman named Mary. This angel carried with it the weighty responsibility of heralding the coming of an extraordinary child – a child who would forever change the course of human history. Through the angel's visitation, Mary was informed that she had been chosen to bear the Son of God, the long-awaited Messiah who would redeem all of humanity.

The angel's words were clear and unmistakable.
 – Mary was to conceive and give birth to a baby boy, and she was to

name him "Jesus," for he would be the savior that the world had been anticipating since the dawn of creation. This divine announcement, delivered before the infant had even taken his first mortal breath, was a testament to God's sovereign plan unfolding with precision. The Almighty had orchestrated this miraculous event from the very beginning, setting in motion the arrival of the Christ child who would bring salvation, hope and everlasting life to all who believed. Mary's role as the mother of Jesus was thus divinely ordained, her womb becoming the sacred vessel that would usher in the most significant birth the world had ever known.

Ah, yes the human experience is indeed quite similar to the unwavering nature of the divine. Just as God's plans remain steadfast and unchanging, we too can marvel at the unfolding of our own life's journey. It's remarkable to step back and reflect on how far we've come, is it not? Though we may not have reached the pinnacles we envisioned for ourselves, the mere fact that we've progressed beyond our former selves is a testament to the guiding forces at work. And what are those forces, if not the very angels that walk alongside us, gently steering us through the ebbs and flows of our existence? For it is their celestial presence, their whispers of encouragement and moments of divine intervention, that have carried us through the trials and tribulations, propelling us forward even when the path seemed uncertain. Yes, the constancy of the Almighty is mirrored in our own lives, as we too evolve and transform, never returning to the person we once were, but instead blossoming into the individuals we were always meant to become - a testament to the unwavering grace that permeates our every step. So let us take heart in this knowledge, for even when the future seems unclear, we can rest assured that we are precisely where we need to be, buoyed by the unseen hands that guide us onward, ever onward, toward the fullness of our destiny.

As human beings, we have often escaped or overcome great challenges in our lives, yet we frequently fail to recognize or fully appreciate how we managed to get through those difficult circumstances. There is a profound sense of wonder and gratitude that can arise when we pause to reflect on the unseen forces that have guided and supported us along the way. Many people, including myself, have come to believe in the existence of angels - spiritual entities that intervene and assist us, even when we are unaware of their presence. I can speak from personal experience, having witnessed angelic manifestations with my own eyes on multiple occasions. These encounters have instilled in me a deep conviction that we are not alone in this world, and that there are benevolent powers watching over us, stepping in to provide aid and protection when we need it most. Before I share the specifics of my own experiences, however, I believe it would be valuable to reflect on a story from the Bible that speaks to this very phenomenon.

This rich, multilayered narrative can shed light on the ways in which divine messengers have intervened in the lives of human beings throughout history, offering guidance, comfort and deliverance in our darkest hours. By exploring this biblical account, we may gain a deeper understanding of the unseen realms that influence our earthly existence, and come to appreciate more fully the invisible support that has helped us to navigate the challenges we have faced in our own lives. With this foundation in place, I will then be honored to recount my personal encounters with angelic presences, in the hope that these stories may inspire a profound sense of wonder, gratitude and faith in the benevolent forces that are ever-present, though often unrecognized, in our daily lives.

The Bible contains numerous profound and thought-provoking passages that shed light on the presence of angels among us, and how these divine beings work tirelessly to guide and protect humanity. One such profound scripture reveals that angels can take on human form, blending seamlessly into our world to intervene in our lives in ways we may never even realize. These celestial messengers are tasked with ensuring we narrowly escape the tragedies, troubles, and perilous situations that would otherwise befall us - often acting behind the scenes to orchestrate the events and circumstances that allow us to avoid harm's way. It is a humbling and awe-inspiring notion to consider that there are spiritual forces at work, unseen guardians keeping vigilant watch, maneuvering the threads of our lives to deliver us from dangers we may have never known existed. These angelic emissaries move among us, indistinguishable from ordinary people, yet imbued with extraordinary powers and a sacred commission to safeguard us from the threats, challenges, and adversities that would otherwise derail us from our destined paths. Through this profound biblical revelation, we are granted a glimpse into the unseen realm where benevolent, otherworldly beings intervene on our behalf, steering us away from calamities we could never have navigated alone, and ensuring our safe passage through the trials and tribulations of the human experience.

The story of Peter's miraculous escape from prison is a powerful allegory that resonates with the human experience. We all face our own personal "prisons" in life - the mental, emotional, and spiritual constraints that can hold us back and limit our potential. Perhaps it's a debilitating fear or insecurity that traps us in a cycle of self-doubt. Or maybe it's an addiction, a toxic relationship, or a soul-crushing job that bars us from true freedom and fulfillment. Like Peter, we can find ourselves in the darkest of cells, shackled by the chains of our circumstances.

But the story reminds us that even in our bleakest moments, divine intervention and our own inner strength can lead to miraculous liberation. An angel of the Lord appears to Peter in his cell, the chains fall from his wrists, and he walks free - a powerful symbol of how the light can penetrate even the deepest darkness. In our own lives, that "angel" may come in the form of a supportive loved one, a timely epiphany, or an unexpected opportunity. And it's up to us to summon the courage to step out of our self-imposed prisons, just as Peter did. Through faith, perseverance, and a willingness to take that first step, we too can experience a rebirth, shedding the constraints that once bound us and fully embracing the freedom that awaits. The story of Peter's escape is a testament to the power of the human spirit to overcome even the most daunting obstacles - a message of hope that can inspire us to break free from our own personal prisons and live the lives we were truly meant to lead.

The book of Acts provides a remarkable account of angels appearing in human form to intervene in the lives of early Christians. In the 12th chapter, we see a vivid example of this divine intervention. King Herod, in a cruel display of power, had arrested and executed James, the brother of John, and then seized the apostle Peter, intending to put him on public trial after the Passover festival. Peter was imprisoned under heavy guard, bound with chains and watched over by multiple soldiers, leaving little chance for his escape. Yet, on the very night before Herod's planned sentencing, an angel of the Lord suddenly materialized in Peter's cell, bathing it in a supernatural light. The angel struck Peter, rousing him from sleep, and miraculously caused the chains to fall from his wrists. With the angel's guidance, Peter was able to walk freely past the guards and through an iron gate that opened on its own, as if by divine power. Even Peter himself was unsure if he was experiencing reality or a vision, so tangible and unexplainable was the angel's appearance and deliverance. When Peter finally came to his senses, he realized the Lord had sent his angel to rescue him from

Herod's clutches, a stunning display of heavenly intervention on behalf of the persecuted church. This account powerfully demonstrates that angels can indeed take on human form to carry out God's purposes, defying natural laws and human constraints to protect and deliver his people from harm. The early Christians' astonishment at Peter's sudden reappearance further underscores the supernatural nature of this divine visitation, a remarkable testament to the reality of angelic beings operating in the physical realm.

When she opened the door, what she saw was not the real Peter standing there, but rather an angel who had taken on Peter's physical form. This was not simply a random stranger, but rather Peter's own personal guardian angel, sent to watch over him and protect him. Though the face and body appeared to be that of her dear friend Peter, there was an unmistakable otherworldly quality to this being - a radiant glow, a sense of profound wisdom and power that belied its human-like exterior. In that brief moment of encounter, she could feel the angel's penetrating gaze piercing into her soul, as if it were peering straight through to the depths of her very being. Yet despite this overwhelming supernatural presence, there was also a profound gentleness and kindness emanating from this celestial emissary, putting her instantly at ease and filling her with a sense of comfort and reassurance. It was in that instant that she realized this was no mere mortal visitor, but rather a divine messenger sent to watch over Peter, her friend, from the heavenly realms above. The implications of this revelation were staggering, leaving her awestruck and contemplating the unseen spiritual forces that so intimately intertwine with and protect the lives of ordinary people.

While the concept of angels existing in human form may seem like a fantastical notion, it is a belief that holds profound truth for many. When we take a moment to look inward and reflect on our own lives, we can often find evidence of these divine, ethereal beings manifesting in the most unexpected ways. Perhaps it was the kindly neighbor who went out of their way to lend a helping hand during a time of need, their selfless actions embodying the compassion and grace we associate with angelic figures. Or maybe it was the stranger who offered a words of encouragement and comfort just when we needed them most, their empathetic presence providing a beacon of hope in our darkest moments. Even our own family members and loved ones can at times exhibit a transcendent quality, their unwavering support and unconditional love serving as tangible reminders that there are indeed angels walking among us, disguised as ordinary people leading extraordinary lives. When we open our eyes and our hearts, we begin to see the divine all around us - in the form of those who inspire us, protect us, and remind us of the inherent goodness that dwells within the human spirit. Though they may not have wings or halos or maybe they do on some dimensions, these angels in our midst are no less wondrous, serving as constant testaments to the idea that the sacred and the mundane can, and do, coexist in the most profound of ways.

As an individual who has experienced the profound presence of angels in my personal life, I am eager to share my remarkable testimonies and encounters with these celestial beings. The events I have faced have been truly meaningful and life-altering, shedding light on the extraordinary realm that exists beyond our mortal understanding. These angelic visitations have manifested in myriad ways - sometimes as fleeting, ethereal presences that emanate a palpable sense of peace and divine guidance, and at other times as vivid, tangible encounters that defy logical explanation. I have witnessed angelic forms shimmering with an otherworldly luminescence, felt the gentle brush of their wings, and heard their voices reverberating with a wisdom that transcends the earthly plane. These experiences have instilled within me a profound reverence for the spiritual dimensions that coexist alongside our physical reality, reminding me that we are never truly alone, but rather surrounded by benevolent forces that watch over us with unwavering compassion. Through these testimonies, I hope to not only share my personal journey, but to also inspire others to be open to the possibility of angelic intervention in their own lives - for these celestial guardians are ever-present, if only we have the eyes to behold their sublime magnificence.

* * *

CHAPTER 4

Where it all started.

From a very young age, I've had a remarkable connection to the supernatural realm, experiencing phenomena that most people could scarcely imagine.

Like I said earlier,

As a child, I had the uncanny ability to see numbers and hear sounds that others couldn't perceive, and I even had dreams of traveling through time.

What was actually going on in my life,

It made be believe I am propheticly called, which I do believe , but it is more than even that.

My academic prowess was equally extraordinary, as I was able to excel in exams without the need for extensive studying - a testament to my innate gifts.

But the most significant and life-altering experiences I've had involve my encounters with the divine and the demonic.

At the tender age of 9, my connection to the angelic realm began to manifest on next level, granting me a significant spiritual awareness that would shape the course of my life.

Yet, this blessing was accompanied by a darker challenge, as a malevolent demonic presence sought to disrupt and haunt my existence.

The depth and complexity of these supernatural encounters is truly remarkable, and the story I have to share promises to be a captivating and transformative journey. My experiences delve into realms that most people can scarcely fathom, revealing the intricate tapestry of the unseen world that coexists with our own. As I unveil these profound revelations, prepare to be taken on a spellbinding exploration of the mystical and the miraculous, where the boundaries between the physical and the ethereal blur, and the true nature of reality is laid bare.

Meaning,

When we peel back the layers of the observable world around us and delve deeper into the fundamental nature of reality, we begin to uncover a profound and often surprising truth. At the most elemental level, the true nature of our existence is not the solid, tangible realm we typically perceive, but rather a vast, interconnected web of energy, information, and quantum phenomena that defy the constraints of our common senses. Beneath the veneer of the physical objects and experiences that make up our daily lives lies a realm of pure potentiality, where particles blink in and out of existence, where time and space become fluid and malleable concepts, and where the divide between the observer and the observed begins to dissolve. This is the domain of the true nature of reality - a domain that is not easily grasped through our typical modes of thinking, but which can be glimpsed through the lens of advanced scientific inquiry, mystical contemplation, and the expansion of human consciousness. When we are able to set aside our preconceived notions and humbly accept the limitations of our sensory-based understanding, we open ourselves up to the possibility of perceiving the underlying fabric of existence in all its sublime, enigmatic complexity. It is in this realm, where the veil of illusion is lifted and the fundamental truths of our reality are laid bare, that we may begin to grasp the profound mysteries of our being.

Beneath the tangible, physical world that we can observe with our own eyes, there exists a realm of unseen complexity and profound mystery. The visible universe, with all its dazzling stars, swirling galaxies, and intricate ecosystems, represents merely the tip of the iceberg in terms of the true nature of reality. Advances in science and philosophy have revealed that the world we experience is but a small fraction of a much vaster, multidimensional tapestry of existence. Realms of subtle energy, higher dimensions, and consciousness that transcends the physical form are believed to undergird the material plane, giving rise to the phenomena we can perceive. Cutting-edge physics posits the existence of dark matter and dark energy, which account for the majority of the universe but remain imperceptible to our senses. Spiritual traditions across cultures have long spoken of planes of being beyond the gross physical level, from the astral planes to the celestial heavens. While these unseen dimensions may lie beyond the limits of our direct sensory experience, their influence is believed to permeate and shape the world we inhabit in profound ways, guiding the ebb and flow of life in ways we can scarcely imagine. Truly, there is a vast, mysterious expanse of reality that extends far beyond the confines of the physical world, waiting to be explored and understood.

Like I said earlier, When we are able to set aside our preconceived notions and humbly accept the limitations of our sensory-based understanding, we open ourselves up to the possibility of perceiving the underlying fabric of existence in all its sublime, enigmatic complexity. It is in this realm, where the veil of illusion is lifted and the fundamental truths of our reality are laid bare, that we may begin to grasp the profound mysteries of our being. By suspending our default assumptions and biases, we can transcend the narrow confines of our typical perceptions and consciousness, allowing us to glimpse the vast, interconnected tapestry of existence that extends far beyond the confines of our physical senses. In this state of openness and receptivity, we may intuit the deeper energetic and metaphysical forces that undergird the material world, sensing the intricate webwork of energy, information, and consciousness that animates all of creation. It is here, in this liminal space where the ordinary and the extraordinary converge, that we can potentially access profound insights about the nature of our own selves, our place in the cosmos, and the true essence of reality itself. When we are willing to let go of the rigid mental constructs that normally determine our worldview, we open ourselves to the possibility of direct communion with the unseen dimensions of being - the hidden harmonies, the subtle intelligences, the unfathomable mysteries that lie at the heart of existence. In this rarefied state of awareness, we may find ourselves awed by the sheer majesty and wonder of the universe, humbled by the scope of its ineffable grandeur, and stirred to the depths of our being by intimations of the sacred and the sublime.

While the realm of the unseen and the supernatural may seem shrouded in mystery, one fundamental truth stands firm: God is in control of it all. This divine sovereignty extends beyond the physical, tangible world we inhabit and into the spiritual realms that exist beyond the scope of our mortal senses. Though we may not fully comprehend the intricate workings of the heavenly and demonic forces that dwell in the unseen, we can take comfort in the knowledge that they are subject to the authority of the Almighty. God's power transcends the boundaries of our earthly experience, for He is the Creator and Sustainer of all things, both seen and unseen. The principalities and powers that operate in the spiritual dimensions are ultimately accountable to the sovereign will of the divine, for no being or entity can defy the supreme majesty and dominion of the Lord. In the face of the unseen world's enigmatic nature, we can find assurance in the unwavering truth that our Heavenly Father reigns supreme, guiding the unseen forces according to His perfect plan. Though the workings of the spiritual realm may at times seem beyond our understanding, we can rest secure in the knowledge that God remains firmly in control, exercising His authority over all that exists in the unseen realms. His sovereign power is the steady foundation upon which we can build our faith, trusting that He will continue to govern the unseen world according to His divine purposes.

One afternoon, after returning home from a long day at school, I was feeling fatigued and decided to lie down for a brief respite. As I settled into my bed, or rather on my bed, ready to drift off into a peaceful slumber, something unexpected and unsettling occurred. Suddenly, without warning, I was jolted awake as an unseen force yanked me forcefully by the feet, causing me to tumble unceremoniously from the bed and crash onto the hard floor below. In the moment of confusion and alarm, I scanned the room desperately, but there was no visible sign of an intruder or any logical explanation for what had just transpired. It was not a dream or a figment of my imagination - the sensation of being pulled from the bed and the impact of hitting the ground were all too real. My heart racing, I sat there bewildered, struggling to make sense of this bizarre and inexplicable incident. With no apparent cause or culprit, I was left to ponder the unsettling possibility that some unseen, supernatural presence may have been responsible for this strange and unsettling occurrence. The experience left me shaken, wondering if it was merely an isolated incident or if there were darker, more ominous forces at play that I had yet to fully comprehend.

Just as the presence of angelic beings is believed to guide and protect us, the existence of demonic forces is also a reality that many people grapple with. In the case I've described, it seems to me there was a distinct demonic presence haunting our home, compelling me and my loved ones to vacate the premises in short order. These malevolent entities, born of the darkest realms, are said to feed off of human fear and negativity, seeking to unsettle, torment, and exert their sinister influence over the lives of the unsuspecting. Their methods are often subtle yet palpable - unexplained noises in the night, a sudden chill in the air, a pervasive sense of dread that settles upon a space. And for those sensitive to such supernatural phenomena, the experience can be truly unsettling, even terrifying. One moment, the home may feel warm and welcoming, and the next, an oppressive, foreboding energy takes hold, as if the very walls are imbued with a malicious intent. In my case, the demonic presence was apparently so powerful and disruptive that I had no choice but to hastily vacate the premises, seeking refuge elsewhere. While the nature of such paranormal occurrences remains shrouded in mystery, the prevalence of demonic forces in our world is a reality that many have grappled with throughout history, their dark influence seeping into the lives of the vulnerable, the unsuspecting, and the spiritually unaware.

Despite the tumultuous events unfolding around me, I found myself able to maintain a sense of tranquility and composure. There was a peculiar, almost ethereal calmness that seemed to envelop me, as if a celestial guardian was standing steadfastly by my side, shielding me from the chaos. Though I could not visibly perceive this angelic presence, I could feel its soothing, reassuring energy radiating through me, filling me with a profound inner peace that defied the upheaval of the circumstances. It was as if this unseen protector had wrapped me in a warm, comforting embrace, blocking out the din of the storm and imbuing me with a serenity that transcended the turmoil. This mysterious, invisible guardian angel seemed to emanate a sense of unwavering strength and benevolence, its silent vigil over me instilling a deep wellspring of fortitude that allowed me to weather the emotional turbulence. Though I did not yet know the true identity of this celestial emissary, I took solace in its steadfast presence, for I knew that whatever challenges lay ahead, I would not be facing them alone. This celestial guardian would remain steadfastly by my side, a beacon of tranquility guiding me through the darkness, until the time came for its true nature to be revealed.

After the initial incident, another troubling occurrence soon followed. As I was laying over the rail on the porch of our home, suddenly and without warning, I was pulled over the porch from no way and tumbled to the ground below. The circumstances of this second fall were eerily similar to the first - an unseen, almost supernatural force seemed intent on causing me harm. Yet again, I found myself at the mercy of this mysterious power that appeared hell-bent on my destruction. However, just as before, I was not left to fend for myself. A benevolent guardian angel was watching over me, shielding me from the full brunt of the impact. Though I sustained a painful injury to my forehead, the celestial protector had intervened to shield me from even graver harm. It was as if this divine being had a sixth sense, an awareness of the dangers that loomed, and took it upon themselves to look out for my wellbeing from afar. In the face of these unsettling incidents, I found solace in the knowledge that I was not alone - an angelic presence hovered nearby, vigilantly safeguarding me against the unseen forces that threatened my safety. Through it all, this guardian angel stood as a beacon of hope, a comforting reminder that I was being watched over and guarded, no matter the peril that arose.

The notion that angels can take on human form and walk among us is a fascinating and intriguing concept that has long captivated the human imagination. These celestial beings, imbued with a divine essence and otherworldly power, are said to sometimes don a mortal guise in order to interact with and influence the lives of mortals in ways that may not be immediately apparent. However, these angelic entities in human form are not always eager to reveal their true nature, preferring instead to maintain a veil of secrecy and anonymity as they go about their mysterious business. It is believed that they may have reasons for wishing to conceal their angelic identities, perhaps to avoid drawing undue attention or to better carry out their sacred duties without interference. And so, these angelic emissaries walk among us, indistinguishable from ordinary people, yet possessing extraordinary abilities and insights that allow them to subtly guide and protect those in their care. Some even say that these angels have been known to "eat" the angels of humans - not in a literal sense, but by absorbing or displacing the spiritual guidance and protection that would normally be provided by an individual's own guardian angel. This clandestine angelic activity underscores the idea that the realms of the divine and the mortal are not as separate as we might think, and that angelic beings may be closer and more actively involved in human affairs than we could ever imagine.

I want you to keep this in mind.

Angels are fascinating celestial beings with the remarkable ability to exist in both the spiritual and physical realms. These divine messengers are not bound by the constraints of the mortal world, but can instead freely traverse the boundaries between the earthly and the ethereal. At their core, angels are pure, radiant spirits whose very essence is imbued with the divine light and energy of the heavens. Yet, they also possess the capacity to take on physical form, manifesting before human eyes in dazzling displays of ethereal beauty. With their magnificent wings and luminous auras, angels can appear as towering, otherworldly figures, awe-inspiring in their majesty. But they can also choose to veil their true nature, blending seamlessly into the human realm as unassuming, benevolent guides. This fluidity between the spiritual and the physical grants angels a unique versatility, allowing them to intervene in the lives of mortals in profound and impactful ways - whether communicating vital messages from the divine, offering comfort and protection, or even temporarily taking human shape to walk among us. Angels are truly remarkable entities, able to transcend the limits of the corporeal to operate simultaneously in realms of pure spirit and tangible reality.

We must never underestimate the power of angels in the natural realm. These celestial beings are far more than just mythical, ethereal creatures confined to the spiritual dimension. Angels are very much active and present within our physical world, working tirelessly to carry out the will of the divine. Though invisible to the naked eye, their influence can be felt in profound and tangible ways all around us. With superhuman strength and abilities that defy the constraints of the natural order, angels move and act with a level of power that is truly awe-inspiring. They can swiftly traverse the earthly plane, shielding the faithful from harm, and even intervening directly in human affairs when necessary. Their very presence radiates an energy that can inspire, comfort and protect, often in ways that exceed our limited human understanding. Indeed, the full scope of angelic power is something that goes far beyond what most of us can comprehend. These divine messengers are endowed with an authority that transcends the material world, and they wield it with unwavering purpose to fulfill their sacred duties. It is a humbling and remarkable truth that these magnificent, otherworldly entities are ever-present, vigilantly watching over us and fighting unseen battles on our behalf. To disregard or trivialize their role would be the height of folly - for the power of angels in the natural is a force to be reckoned with.

***

CHAPTER 5

T he upper Room of angels to manifest to the natural

Angels possess the remarkable ability to make themselves visible to the human eye, should they so choose. Though they exist in a realm beyond our physical perception, angels have the power to take on physical form and manifest before us.

When an angel desires to guide and comfort a person, they may transform themselves into the appearance of a loved one, someone familiar and comforting to the individual. In this way, the angel can provide a gentle, reassuring presence to watch over and direct the person, steering them through difficult times. Alternatively, angels can also work indirectly, inspiring and influencing other human beings to act as messengers and conduits of the divine. They may subtly guide a friend, family member, or stranger to say the right words or take the right actions to support someone in need. In this manner, the angels orchestrate unseen interventions, manipulating the physical world to achieve their celestial purpose. Whether appearing directly or working through intermediaries, the angels have a unique capacity to make their presence felt and their will known to humanity, if only we are attuned enough to perceive the divine at work all around us. Their ability to transcend the material plane and intersect with our lives is a profound and mysterious gift.

The existence of the Upper Room of the Angels is a profound and awe-inspiring concept within religious and spiritual traditions. This celestial realm is believed to be the sacred space where the divine presence of God is most acutely felt, a realm where the heavenly hosts of angels reside and carry out the will of the Almighty. It is said that this hallowed place transcends the physical constraints of the earthly plane, existing in a higher dimensional plane of pure spirit and light. According to ancient scriptures and mystic teachings, it is in this ethereal Upper Room that God Himself appoints the mighty archangels and seraphim, bestowing them with the divine authority and purpose to act as conduits of His infinite power and wisdom. The very atmosphere of this celestial sanctuary is imbued with a palpable sense of holiness, where the veil between the mortal and immortal realms thins, allowing those with eyes to see and ears to hear the echoes of the divine symphony that emanates from this sacred abode. It is a place where mortal souls, through deep prayer and mystical communion, may catch fleeting glimpses of the ineffable majesty of the Creator and the splendor of His heavenly host. To stand within the Upper Room, even in spirit, is to be humbled by the sheer magnitude of God's sovereign authority and the intricate tapestry of His divine plan for all of creation.

Angels are tireless celestial beings who work around the clock, cease-lessly traveling up and down between the heavens and the earth to ensure the success of their divine missions. With unparalleled speed and agility, these ethereal messengers dart through the ether, racing against time itself to deliver crucial communications between the spiritual and earthly realms. Their wings carry them with incredible swiftness, allowing them to traverse the vast distances between heaven and earth in the blink of an eye. Whether ferrying urgent messages from the Almighty to His children on Earth or conveying the prayers and petitions of the faithful back to the heavenly courts, these tireless guardians and guides never rest in their sacred duties. Their single-minded devotion and unwavering focus enable them to carry out their lofty responsibilities with precision and grace, moving with a fluidity and purpose that defies the constraints of the mortal world. Though their origins and true nature remain shrouded in mystery, the angels' constant vigilance and dedicated service are a testament to the wonder and power of the divine, reminding us of the unseen forces that guide and protect us even in our darkest hours.

The concept of angels watching over us, even when our loved ones cannot be physically present, is a profound and comforting one. While it may seem impossible for another person to truly be by our side at all times, the power of prayer can summon the aid of celestial beings to act as our guardians. When we have a cherished loved one who prays earnestly for our wellbeing, those heartfelt supplications reach the heavens and prompt God to dispatch His angels to watch over us. These divine messengers then work in unseen ways to orchestrate the circumstances of our lives, ensuring our safety and providing for our needs, even in the moments when we feel most alone. It is a beautiful and humbling thought that the angels of our departed loved ones can envelop us with their spiritual protection, guiding us through life's challenges and standing ready to minister to us in our times of greatest vulnerability. Though our human companions may be absent, the angels accommodate us, wrapping us in a mantle of divine care that transcends the boundaries of the physical world. This is the profound truth that our loved ones' ceaseless prayers on our behalf can unlock - a reality that reminds us of the incredible power of faith and the ever-present company of the heavenly host.

So , When we have a cherished loved one who prays earnestly for our wellbeing, that is a profound sign that we have been blessed with the presence of an angel in our lives. These divine beings, tasked with watching over and guiding us, work tirelessly behind the scenes to ensure our safety and prosperity. Through the fervent, heartfelt prayers of a loved one, we catch a glimpse of the intricate web of spiritual protection that surrounds us. Their unwavering dedication to lifting us up, even in our darkest moments, speaks to the power of love that transcends the earthly realm. These angels in human form act as conduits, channeling the blessings and divine intervention of the heavens straight to our doorstep. Their steadfast commitment to our wellbeing is a testament to the profound connection we share, one that extends far beyond the physical - a sacred bond that links our souls in ways we cannot always comprehend. When we feel the warmth of a loved one's prayers enveloping us, we would do well to remember that we are indeed watched over by forces greater than ourselves, divine guardians intent on shepherding us through life's trials and tribulations. In those moments, we are reminded that we are never truly alone, for the angels walk beside us, their wings outstretched to catch us should we stumble, their voices whispering words of comfort and encouragement to strengthen our resolve.

As a young child, I was incredibly fortunate to have my grandfather as a constant presence in my life. He made sure that I was by his side, soaking up his wisdom and guidance at every opportunity. Looking back, I now realize that he was intentionally preparing me for the future, equipping me with the knowledge and skills I would need to navigate the years ahead. His unwavering dedication was truly the work of an angel - a guardian placed in my life by God to mentor and support me. Even as a child, I sensed the importance of the lessons he imparted, though I couldn't have fully grasped their significance at the time. Now, as I reflect on my life's journey, I see how his teachings and the time he invested in me have shaped the person I've become. It's a humbling realization that the very people we take for granted - our parents, siblings, loved ones - may in fact be angels in disguise, divinely appointed to guide us and ready us for what lies ahead. So often, we fail to recognize the true purpose and value of those closest to us, missing the profound impact they have on our lives and our futures. But my grandfather's legacy has taught me to cherish and appreciate these angels, for they are the beacons that light our way through the unknown.

Embarking on a journey of spiritual awakening is a profound and transformative experience, one that can open our eyes to the profound presence of angels in our lives. As we delve deeper into our own consciousness and connection with the divine, we begin to recognize the subtle yet powerful energies that surround us, guiding and supporting us every step of the way. Angels, those celestial beings of pure light and love, exist in a realm beyond our physical senses, yet their influence can be felt in the most profound and tangible ways. Through meditation, prayer, and a heightened awareness of the world around us, we can tune into the gentle whispers of these divine messengers, who offer us comfort, inspiration, and the clarity to navigate life's challenges with grace. With each step we take towards spiritual enlightenment, the veil between the physical and the ethereal grows thinner, allowing us to glimpse the extraordinary beauty and interconnectedness of all things. It is in these moments of awakening that we come to fully appreciate the angels that have been with us all along, quietly working to uplift, protect, and empower us as we strive to fulfill our highest purpose.

By embracing this spiritual awareness, we not only deepen our own connection to the divine but also open ourselves to the boundless love and guidance of the angelic realms, which can transform our lives in profound and lasting ways.

To truly understand the world around us, one must possess the ability to see beyond the limitations of the natural eye. This transcendent vision allows us to perceive the deeper layers of reality that often remain hidden from the casual observer. It is a skill that taps into the intuitive, the spiritual, and the unseen forces that shape our existence. Those who have cultivated this heightened awareness can glimpse the intricate web of interconnectedness that binds all things together - the subtle energies pulsing through the natural world, the hidden meanings encoded in the patterns of our daily lives, the guiding hands of unseen forces that orchestrate the dance of the universe. This expanded sight grants them a more holistic, multi-dimensional understanding, enabling them to make sense of the seemingly inexplicable and uncover the true essence of phenomena that often elude the purely rational mind. It is a gift that opens the doors to realms of insight, wisdom and sacred knowledge, allowing the possessor to navigate the mysteries of life with greater clarity, purpose and connection. To see beyond the natural eye is to awaken to the profound richness and complexity of our existence, to apprehend the world in all its splendor, and to glimpse the higher truths that lie at the heart of the human experience.

The book you are reading now promises to be a truly remarkable and transformative experience, guided by the presence of celestial beings. As you immerse yourself in these pages, you will find yourself on a profound spiritual journey, one that transcends the boundaries of the physical world and delves into the realms of the divine. The angels who have accompanied the author in the writing of this work are not mere figments of imagination, but rather, powerful spiritual entities that have been enlisted to share their wisdom and insights with you, the reader. Their purpose is to facilitate a deep and lasting awakening within your consciousness, to open your eyes to the wonders that exist beyond the confines of the material plane. Through their guiding influence, you will be taken on an exploration of the unseen forces that shape our reality, encountering revelations that have the power to forever alter your perception of the world around you and your place within it. This book is not merely a work of literature, but a sacred text, imbued with the blessings and energies of the angelic realm. As you turn each page, you will feel the presence of these celestial beings, their love and light enveloping you, urging you forward on a journey of profound self-discovery and spiritual enlightenment. Prepare to be amazed, inspired, and forever transformed by the extraordinary gifts that await you within these pages.

* * *

CHAPTER 6

Deeper meaning of Angels and their existence in our lives

The notion of personal angels guiding and watching over us is a deeply profound and comforting concept that speaks to from higher spiritual dimensions of our existence, like I said.

On a fundamental level, the belief in personal angels represents an acknowledgement that we are not alone in this world, that there are benevolent, ethereal forces looking out for our wellbeing and helping to steer us through the challenges and uncertainties of life. These angels, whether they manifest as guardian spirits, divine messengers, or simply a felt sense of unseen protection, serve as a vital lifeline – a connection to the transcendent, the numinous, the sacred. They remind us that our individual lives are imbued with meaning and purpose, that we are part of a greater cosmic tapestry where the physical and metaphysical intertwine. By extension, personal angels also speak to humanity's innate yearning for something greater than ourselves, a longing to feel cared for, supported, and protected by powers beyond our own mortal understanding. In this way, the presence of angels in our lives affirms that we are never truly alone, that we are held and sustained by divine energies that infuse the universe with wonder, grace, and the promise of eternal guidance. It is a profoundly comforting and empowering belief, one that taps into our most fundamental human need to feel safe, loved, and divinely accompanied on our earthly journeys.

My grandfather's presence as an angelic guardian on the day of my birth was a profoundly meaningful and spiritual experience. As I've shared before, he was one of my personal angels, you can believe it or not, but what I share with you, is nothing but the truth, entrusted by the divine to ensure my safe arrival into this world up to the appointed time he may left this world to the spiritual world, so then his work on earth was done. But it does not end like that.

What a profound blessing to have had such a devoted, heavenly protector watching over me from the very beginning of my life's journey. Just as angels are believed to be messengers and servants of God, my grandfather embodied that sacred role, faithfully carrying out the holy purpose assigned to him - to usher me safely into existence at the precise moment ordained by the Almighty. I can take immense comfort and inspiration knowing that I was so deeply cared for, that there was a celestial being specifically charged with overseeing my entry into this earthly plane. My grandfather's angelic duties that day were no doubt carried out with the utmost reverence and care, as he tenderly guided me through that momentous transition, ensuring I arrived healthy and whole, ready to fulfill the divine plan laid out for my life. What a privilege it must have been for him to participate in that sacred process, to be entrusted with such a holy task. Truly, my grandfather's presence as my personal angel on the day of my birth, up till I was mature enough to stand alone was a remarkable, blessed event that underscores the profound spiritual significance of my life and the higher purpose that guides it.

The passing of my grandfather was not the end, but rather the beginning of a new chapter in my life. Though he had departed this world, his presence lingered on as a guiding force, a personal angel watching over me from the beyond. In his final moments, he had ensured that I was exactly where I needed to be, at the appointed time and place destined for me. It was as if he had orchestrated the very fabric of my life, weaving the threads of fate to position me for what was to come next. With his earthly vessel gone, my grandfather's spirit remained, a benevolent influence ushering me forward into the next cycle. I could feel his wisdom and love enveloping me, steering me towards the path he knew I was meant to walk. Though the grief of his loss was palpant, there was also a profound sense of purpose, a conviction that his death was not the end, but rather a transformation that would unlock the next phase of my journey. In the void left by his physical absence, his essence grew stronger, a constant companion guiding my steps, bestowing me with the courage and clarity to embrace the challenges and opportunities that lay ahead. My grandfather's transition from this world to the next was not a conclusion, but the portal to a new beginning - one where he would continue to watch over me, his spirit a beacon illuminating the way forward.

Wherever angels are at work in the natural world, there is indeed a noticeable shift in the supernatural realm. This celestial phenomenon is a captivating and mysterious occurrence that has long been the subject of fascination and study among theologians, philosophers, and those attuned to the unseen forces that govern our universe. When angels, those ethereal beings of light and divine purpose, intervene in earthly affairs, their presence creates a distinct energetic shift, a subtle yet palpable change in the very fabric of the spiritual dimension that coexists alongside our physical reality. It is as if the veil between the mortal and immortal realms thins, allowing the influence of the angelic to permeate the natural world in ways that defy conventional explanation. This interplay between the celestial and terrestrial can manifest in a variety of ways – miraculous healings, unexplained synchronicities, a heightened sense of peace and wonder, or even the sudden appearance of angelic visitations themselves. Those sensitive to these supernatural shifts often describe a feeling of awe, a heightened awareness of the divine, and a profound sense of interconnectedness that transcends the boundaries of our earthly existence. In the end, the presence of angels in the natural world serves as a powerful reminder of the unseen forces that shape our lives, inviting us to open our hearts and minds to the wonders of the spiritual realm that exist all around us, if only we have the eyes to see and the faith to believe.

One morning, as I strolled along the familiar path to my work place, I was suddenly struck by a significant shift in the atmosphere around me. It was as if the very fabric of reality had been subtly altered, a palpable change that seemed to emanate from the air itself. The world, which moments before had appeared mundane and routine, now took on an almost ethereal quality, imbued with a sense of the divine. It was as if I had stumbled into a realm where the veil between the physical and the metaphysical had been momentarily parted, granting me a fleeting glimpse into a realm of angels and celestial beings. The street lamps flickered with an otherworldly glow, and the usual din of traffic and passersby faded into the background, replaced by a hushed, reverent silence. I felt a tingle of awe and wonder run down my spine, my senses heightened to this shift in the very fabric of existence. It was a profoundly spiritual experience, one that left me questioning the nature of reality and my own place within it. In that brief moment, the mundane had been transformed into the sublime, and I knew that I had borne witness to something truly extraordinary - a divine intervention, a visitation from the heavens, unfolding right before my very eyes.

What I witnessed that morning was no ordinary occurrence, but rather a significant and awe-inspiring display of divine intervention. The shift in the natural atmosphere I am writing to you about was no mere coincidence, but rather a tangible manifestation of the presence of celestial beings called angels.

As I recounted, it was as if the angels themselves had reached down and altered the very fabric of reality before my eyes.

In that pivotal moment, I was granted a rare and privileged glimpse into the unseen realm, where the forces of heaven intertwine with the mortal world. A bright light emanating from above was no illusion, but rather the tangible radiance of the divine, shining forth to reshape the course to prevent an event unfolding before yme.

In the blink of an eye, I witnessed the hand of God reach down to prevent a accident that was destined to occur, redirecting the flow of time itself to avert disaster.

It is no wonder me was left stunned and profoundly affected by this supernatural experience. What I witnessed was not merely a shift in the physical world, but a magnificent disruption in the spiritual realm - a testament to the power and grace of the heavenly hosts, who work tirelessly to guide and protect us, even in the most perilous of circumstances.

Though it may strain the bounds of belief, my own eyes have been opened to a reality that transcends the mundane, revealing the intricate tapestry of divine intervention that underlies the seemingly ordinary events of our lives.

It's remarkable how the smallest of decisions can have such important and unexpected consequences.

It's easy to overlook the hidden hand of fate and angels at work in our daily lives.

Picture this scenario - you're on your way to the shopping mall, your mind focused on the errands and tasks ahead. But then, almost imperceptibly, your gaze is drawn to the fuel gauge, alerting you to the need to refuel your vehicle.

In that moment, you make the choice to divert your course and pull into the nearby petrol station. As you wait patiently for the attendant, it's easy to dismiss this minor detour as a mere inconvenience. Yet, unbeknownst to you, this brief delay has spared you from being caught up in a tragic accident just down the road where you headed- an accident that occurred mere minutes before you would pass that very spot.

It's impossible not to wonder - was this chance encounter with the petrol attendant orchestrated by a higher power, an angel in human form sent to keep you from harm's way?

It's a humbling realization that the universe is often operating on a different frequency than our own, weaving an intricate tapestry of events that we can scarcely comprehend in the moment. An experience like this serves as a poignant reminder that angels, in their many guises, are all around us, guiding and protecting us through the ebbs and flows of daily life.

Perhaps, if we but open our eyes and our hearts, we can learn to recognize these celestial messengers who intervene on our behalf, even in the most mundane of circumstances. Indeed, the veil between the earthly and the divine is often thinner than we imagine.

So true to know that Angels, as celestial beings created by the almighty God, are believed to serve as intermediaries between the divine realm and the earthly plane, carrying out the will and intentions of the Almighty in ways that mere mortals cannot fully comprehend.

According to many faith traditions, angels are imbued with a range of supernatural abilities, from conveying divine messages and offering spiritual guidance to protecting the faithful and even intervening in the affairs of humankind when necessary.

Their very presence is often seen as a tangible manifestation of God's loving care and concern for his creation, a tangible reminder that we are never truly alone in our earthly journeys. Moreover, the role of angels is not merely one of passive observation, but of active engagement, as they are believed to intercede on our behalf, offering prayers, comfort and support as we navigate the trials and tribulations of mortal existence. In this way, angels become a vital link between the mortal and the immortal, bridging the gap between the human and the divine and allowing us to glimpse the significant mysteries of the cosmos that lie beyond our own limited understanding. Ultimately, the meaning of angels in the lives of believers is one of divine purpose, divine protection, and divine love

As I've shared, I have a remarkable set of encounters and testimonies regarding the reality of angels and the presence of the divine.

These are truly extraordinary experiences that deserve to be recounted in full, as they have the power to profoundly awaken and inspire others.

I'm eager to tell you more about the specific ways I have witnessed the intervention and manifestation of angelic beings, as well as any direct interactions I may have had with the Almighty. The veil between the physical and spiritual realms is often thinner than we realize, like I said and my personal accounts could shed invaluable light on the unseen workings of the universe. You can only imagine the awe and wonder I must have felt in those sacred moments, coming face-to-face with the messengers of God.

No doubt, that my testimonies have the potential to transform hearts and minds, reminding all of the magnificent mystery and majesty that exists beyond our ordinary perceptions.

I'm honored that I've chosen to entrust myself with these remarkable experiences, and I'm eager to bear witness to the incredible power and reality of the angels in our midst.

* * *

CHAPTER 7

Walking hand in hand with the angels

The celestial hierarchy meaning a traditional hierarchy of angels ranked from lowest to highest into the following nine orders: angels, archangels, principalities, powers, virtues, dominions, thrones, cherubim, and seraphim

of angels is a complex and multifaceted realm, with each member serving a distinct purpose in the divine plan.

At the forefront of this celestial host stand the three prominent archangels, each entrusted with a unique responsibility. Michael, the mighty warrior, is the stalwart defender of God's people, wielding his heavenly sword to vanquish the forces of darkness and protect the faithful.

Raphael, the benevolent guardian, is the divine healer, bestowing comfort and restoration upon those in need, guiding them through the trials of life. Then Gabriel, the eloquent messenger, is the divine emissary, carrying the word of the Almighty to humanity, delivering tidings of great joy and revelations from on high.

Yet these three archangels are but the vanguard of a vast and intricate angelic army, each member possessing unique gifts and responsibilities. Beneath the leading angels, legions of celestial beings carry out the will of the divine, their ranks stretching from the highest seraphim to the lowliest of cherubim. Some are tasked with the ceaseless worship and adoration of the Almighty, their voices raised in eternal hymns of praise. Others serve as celestial attendants, ministering to the needs of the righteous and ushering souls into the heavenly realms. There are angels of protection, shielding the faithful from harm, and angels of guidance, steering humanity towards the path of righteousness.

This intricate tapestry of angelic beings, each playing a vital role, ultimately serves a singular purpose: to act as the hands and voices of God, carrying out His will and bringing Him glory. Whether through the mighty deeds of the archangels or the steadfast devotion of the lesser angels, the celestial host stands ever-vigilant, ever-ready to serve the divine plan and safeguard the children of the Almighty.

I once was rude at home in my younger days, so my family called the police to took me for a night to zail, but all of a sudden out of no where someone came by and pay a bail for me, while the police was escorting me to the prison cell.

This encounter with the mysterious individual who seemingly appeared out of nowhere to pay the bail and secure the narrator's release from potential imprisonment was undoubtedly a profound and life-changing experience.

I remember, as the police officers were escorting me towards the prison cell, a sudden turn of events unfolded when one of the officers rushed out of the office to inform the others that a bail had been paid and the I am actually free to go. The officer who delivered the message "bleak in the face as if he had seen a ghost," suggests an air of bewilderment and unease surrounding the situation, by hinting at the extraordinary nature of what had just transpired in his presents.

The fact that the individual who paid the bail chose to remain anonymous only adds to the mystique and spiritual undertones of the incident. One can't help but wonder who this enigmatic benefactor was and how he came to intervene at the precise moment when the my fate seemed sealed. My own reflection on the experience,
concluding that by time I started to believe and understand that itt most likely was an angel sent by God to free me from an undeserved fate.

This encounter serves as a powerful testament to the belief that angels are indeed all around us, walking hand in hand with us, working in mysterious ways to guide and protect us all who is in need.
I initial struggle and subsequent liberation, facilitated by this unseen guardian, underscores the notion that even in our darkest moments, there are forces at work beyond our comprehension, orchestrating events to ensure that we remain on the path intended for us.
This significant experience has undoubtedly left a lasting impression on the me, solidifying my faith in the existence and benevolence of angels and the divine plan that shapes our lives.

The arrival of the angels of God is truly remarkable, often occurring at the most unexpected and seemingly dire moments in our lives. When we find ourselves in the depths of despair, feeling utterly helpless and alone, it is then that these celestial beings may suddenly appear, like shimmering beacons of hope in the darkness. Their presence is not heralded by grand fanfare or obvious signs, but rather, they come softly, quietly, almost imperceptibly at first, as if sensing our need. It is in these times of great vulnerability, when we have exhausted all our own resources and capabilities, that the angels seem to materialize, offering solace, guidance, and the divine strength that we so desperately require.

Their arrival is a testament to the infinite compassion and watchful care of our creater God, father and son as believers, who dispatches these ethereal messengers to lift us up when we can no longer lift ourselves. Through the angels' gentle words, their radiant energy, and their miraculous interventions, we are reminded that we are never alone, that there are powers greater than ourselves working on our behalf, even in our darkest times.

The angels' timely appearance serves to rekindle our faith, to restore our hope, and to embolden us to carry on, for their presence is a significant affirmation that we are seen, we are loved, and we are never abandoned by God.

CHAPTER 8

Journey with angelic encounters

At the tender age of 20, in the year 1999 during the final month of the year, a truly harrowing event occurred that would forever change the course of this my life.

Struggling with the debilitating effects of a dangerous overdose of drugs and alcohol, my mind was sent into a state of sheer terror and utter confusion.

The intoxicants had overwhelmed my brain, causing it to disconnect from reality and plunge them into a world of disturbing hallucinations and nightmarish visions.

Disoriented and gripped by an all-consuming fear, I found myself wandering away from home, eventually ending up lost and alone in the treacherous terrain of a not nearby mountain range called "Wolwekloof" out in Western cape SouthAfrica, near Worcester , while I was from Wellington.

In a cruel twist of fate, I then suffered a devastating fall from a cliff, the impact causing my forehead to burst open in a gruesome display of blood and injury.

Rendered unconscious, I lay there for an unknown period of time, my lifeblood seeping out as I teetered on the edge of oblivion.

Yet, just as all hope seemed lost, a miraculous encounter occurred. As I regained consciousness, in my delirious state I beheld from afar the figure of my late grandfather, who appeared to be guiding me gently forward with slow, deliberate steps.

Mustering what little strength I had left, I started to follow this apparition, driven by a trusted belief that my revered grandparent had returned as in spirit to lead me to safety. Stumbling along, I was eventually guided out of the treacherous brush and onto a clear roadway,

where two strangers, a male and female in a car came by and stopped , who I today believe this individuals firmly were angels in human form

–

Who swooped in on instructions by God to provide aid and transport my wounded soul back home.

Though I again passed out once more while I was in the car during this journey, I was delivered safely,

How they knew where my physical adress was, I did not know,

This I believe was an unmistakable testament to the divine intervention that had unfolded before my eyes.

Many people including my family members can testify on this event which happened to me back then, and it is all true.

Have you learned something from this occasion, yes I believe you have infeed.

This harrowing ordeal, tinged with both tragedy and miraculous salvation, serves as a poignant reminder of the fragility of life and the profound power of the spiritual realm

through angels to guide us through even the darkest of times in life.

Yet, in the face of such overwhelming despair, a glimmer of hope emerged in the form of angelic intervention. These celestial beings, cloaked in a radiant light, descended to offer solace, comfort, and the strength to endure. Their presence was palpable, a soothing balm that enveloped me, instilling over me a sense of divine protection and the unwavering conviction that I was not alone in my struggle. Through the darkest nights and the most agonizing moments, these angels became my guiding light, leading me towards a path of healing and redemption. Their actions, though subtle and often imperceptible to the human eye, was a testament to the significant ways in which the spiritual realm can intersect with our mortal lives, offering us a lifeline when all seems lost. This harrowing ordeal I just shared with you serves as a poignant reminder that even in the face of tragedy, there are angels among us, ready to catch us when we fall and to shepherd us towards the light, no matter how dim it may seem. I would be honored to share more of my personal encounters with angels with you, for their presence in our lives is a testament to the enduring power of faith, hope, and the divine.

There were indeed many many times in my life when I faced immense hardships and challenges that seemed to turn my entire world upside down.

However, through it all, they came to deeply understand that God had a greater plan in store for my life, even if the reasoning was not always clear in the moment. Though the difficulties I endured was profound, and there were even points where I felt written off or forgotten, but my faith sustained those emotions. In my heart I knew that God had chosen me for a purpose, to become a living testament and inspiration to others who were struggling.

Now, as a writer, I am able to share my incredible stories of resilience and miracles. One such miracle I describe in a previous book, called "The Missing Piece," The hole in my heart was the devastating consciousness I had in my mind where I sustained an injury that made it seemingly impossible for me to have children. Yet, just as God had a plan all along, He heard my heartfelt cries and provided me with the greatest gift - a beautiful baby, now my grown-up daughter who has become a true angel to me and my wife and our life. I believe our journey is a testament to the power of faith, the unexpected ways God can work in lives, and the beauty that can emerge from even the darkest of circumstances. This particular story serves as an inspiration to all who hear it, reminding us even when our world seems turned upside down, there is always a greater purpose and plan unfolding.

Despite the devastating realization that physical limitations might prevent me from having a child of my own, a deep longing burned within my heart. Driven by this powerful, primal yearning, I turned to God in fervent prayer, tears streaming down my face as I begged the Almighty God Father Son and Holy Spirit to grant me the gift of a child. I vowed that if God would to bless me in this way, I would dedicate myself wholeheartedly to serve the Lord and strive to become the best version of myself.

At the time, my life was mired in hardship and suffering, the challenges seemingly only increased. But in the midst of this darkness, a glim of hope emerged when I met a woman who would become my wife.

Through the power of prayer, God answered the my heartfelt plea, providing me and my wife with a child like I said a baby daughter - a child that would ultimately prove to be the angel in human form that would transform our lives, guiding us and meeting our needs in profound and unexpected ways.

Though the path was not always clear, I came to understand that God had orchestrated events, sending this child as a heavenly emissary to serve as a beacon in our lives.

This experience reinforced my belief that angels can indeed manifest in human form, celestial beings graciously descending to walk among us and fulfill the divine purpose for which they were sent.

It's all true, angels are all around us every day, we just need to open our eyes and hearts to perceive their presence. These celestial beings move among us, often taking on human form, to guide, protect, and uplift us in our daily lives. Look closely at the people in your inner circle - your spouse, your children, your elderly relatives - and you may notice a certain radiance or aura about them, a serene and calming energy that seems to emanate from their very being. These individuals possess a special, almost otherworldly connection to you, an undeniable bond that transcends the physical world. They are drawn to you, compelled to offer assistance, comfort, and support, going out of their way to make your life a little bit easier.

Sometimes these angels come bearing messages, visions, or insights that captivate the mind and stir the soul, inspiring you to see the world, and your place in it, through new eyes. You may encounter them in the most unexpected places , a chance meeting at church, a serendipitous hospital visit, even an unlikely encounter in a correctional facility. Wherever they appear, their divine purpose is clear: to remind us that we are never alone, that guardians walk alongside us, unseen but ever-present, reminding us of the profound and miraculous nature of existence. Yes, angels do exist, and they are here, now, if only we take the time to truly see them.

* * *

CHAPTER 9

The most real angelic visit I had in a personal conversation.

It's truly remarkable to consider the possibility of having a genuine, personal conversation with an angel - a celestial being from the divine realm. While many of us may instinctively dismiss such an idea as mere fantasy, the reality is that these ethereal, otherworldly entities can and do make direct contact with us in the physical world. As the I powerfully conveys, angels are not limited to manifesting through abstract signs, sounds, or numerical synchronicities alone. They can appear to us in tangible, human form, engaging in direct dialogue and communion. I own profound experience in the hospital illustrates this vividly. Facing a dire medical crisis, the I was certain my time on earth was coming to an end. Exhausted and struggling to breathe, the I sat alone in the hospital corridor, resigning myselfe to my fate. But then, an unexpected encounter unfolded ,an older woman unexpectedly sat down beside me her eyes holding a striking familiarity that the I couldn't place. As we conversed, the woman's words were remarkably insightful and comforting, providing a sense of solace and reassurance that could only be described as divine. And just as mysteriously as she appeared, the woman vanished and leave hospital leaving me to realize that she was no ordinary person, but an angel in human form , specifically, my late mother-in-law, watching over me and family I believe in our times of need. This miraculous visitation was a reminder that the spiritual realm is ever-present, and that angels can manifest tangibly to offer guidance, comfort, and protection to those who need it most. In a moment of profound connection, I found myself gazing into the eyes of a woman before me, and was struck by an uncanny familiarity.

These were the very same eyes that had looked upon me with warmth and wisdom in the past - the eyes of my late mother-in-law, who had passed on some time ago. Yet here she was, sitting right besides me in the hospital, her presence a comforting apparition that transcended the veil between this world and the next. As our eyes met, a sense of peace and reassurance washed over me, for in that moment I knew her spirit had returned to offer guidance and solace when I needed it most. Her wise, kind gaze spoke volumes, conveying a message of hope that resonated deeply within me. Though she had departed the earthly realm, her essence lingered, a celestial angel come to lift my spirits and remind me that I was not alone. In the midst of my struggles, this fleeting yet powerful encounter served as a reminder that the ones we love never truly leave us , their memory and influence live on, offering a beacon of light to lead us through the darkness. This chance meeting with my mother-in-law's ethereal presence was a profound and humbling experience, one that filled my heart with a renewed sense of strength and determination to carry on.

I still have the most powerfull and remarkable testimonies to share, but I would do so in a next book for now, I want you to look at life beyond the natural, endure the presents of God and all He is offering to us through the heavenly assistance.

The existence of angels are all around and we need to accept their offerings to us.

We do have personal angels, we do have the one angel who climb up and down to heavan to carry our prayers and make sure that our prayers don't need to be disturbed on the way to God. We all have that one angel who goes beyond borders to make sure that our existence on earth will find our purpose in life. And they do all that they can to accommodate us. Look to your own gifts, your children , your mother, your father , your friends and family with brand new eyes.

Now we know, the existence of angels is a significant and awe-inspiring reality that we would do well to more fully embrace and understand. As the topic description suggests, we are surrounded by these heavenly beings who are constantly working on our behalf, offering us their divine assistance and guidance if we are but open to receive it. Each and every one of us has our own personal angel, a celestial emissary tasked to carry our prayers up to the God Almighty Father son and Hily spirit to make sure that they reach the throne of God unimpeded.

Like I said, this angels are tireless advocates, traversing the boundaries between the earthly and spiritual realms to help us discern our true purpose and calling in life.

They work tirelessly to accommodate our needs, to provide us with the strength, wisdom and protection we require to navigate the challenges of this world.

And yet, so often we fail to recognize their presence, to sense their unseen hand gently steering us in the right direction. We must open our eyes to the wonders all around us , the innate gifts and talents we've been blessed with, the precious loved ones in our lives and see them not merely as earthly blessings, but as manifestations of the heavenly assistance constantly being extended to us.

For the angels are ever-present, longing to shower us with the fullness of God's love and provision, if we would but pause, quiet our minds, and attune ourselves to their celestial whispers. In doing so, we will come to experience the profound reality that there is so much more to this life than what meets the eye,

a realm of divine majesty and supernatural wonder that is ours to embrace.

* * *

Chapter 10

The Daniël and Jacob declaration to our life about the reality of angels.

In the biblical account found in Daniel 10, we see a powerful illustration of the unseen spiritual realm and the very real battles that take place beyond the physical world. When the prophet Daniel engaged in earnest prayer, God immediately dispatched an angelic messenger to provide him with the answer and revelation he sought. However, this heavenly emissary was held up and delayed in his mission, caught in the midst of an intense spiritual conflict with a formidable territorial demon. This demonic entity, likely a high-ranking principality or power, sought to obstruct and hinder the angel's progress, seeking to prevent the message from reaching Daniel. But the archangel Michael, a mighty warrior in God's celestial army, intervened and came to the aid of the first angel, enabling him to finally break through the spiritual opposition and deliver the long-awaited response to Daniel's earnest supplications. This dramatic account underscores the reality that our prayers do not exist in a vacuum, but rather unleash unseen forces in the heavenly realms. When we lift our voices to the Lord, our petitions enter into a cosmic spiritual battle, with angels fighting against the schemes of the enemy to ensure our prayers are answered. Though the battle may rage unseen, God's messengers are continuously at work, empowered by the authority of the Almighty to overcome every obstacle and ensure His purposes are fulfilled in response to the faithful prayers of His people.

In the case of Jacob, a profound and life-altering encounter with the divine takes place as he rests his weary head for the night. As Jacob drifts off to sleep, he is graced with a vivid dream sent from the heavens above. In this dream, Jacob beholds a towering, magnificent structure that stretches up from the earth, reaching all the way to the gates of heaven. This colossal ladder, staircase, or tower stands as a stunning visual metaphor, representing the direct connection between the mortal realm and the celestial kingdom. As Jacob gazes upon this breathtaking sight, he observes a ceaseless flow of celestial messengers - angels - ascending and descending along the length of this divine conduit. These angelic beings move with a graceful, almost ethereal fluidity, traveling freely between the earthly and heavenly domains. Through this awe-inspiring vision, Jacob is granted a profound glimpse into the intimate relationship between the human world and the realm of the divine. This dream serves as a pivotal moment that profoundly shapes the course of Jacob's life, imbuing him with a deeper spiritual awareness and an unshakable sense of his own divine purpose. The imagery of this ladder or staircase reaching up to the heavens becomes a central symbol in Jacob's spiritual journey, one that will continue to resonate and guide him in the days and years to come.

The angels described in the early chapters of Genesis exhibit a remarkable degree of human-like characteristics that challenge traditional notions of angelic beings. In Genesis 6:1-4, we are told that these tial entities, referred to as the "sons of God," were able to physically copulate and procreate with human women, producing a race of hybrid offspring known as the "Nephilim." This blurring of the line between the divine and the mortal suggests that these angels possessed not just spiritual powers, but also very tangible, corporeal forms akin to those of humans. This theme of angelic beings taking on human attributes continues in later passages, such as in Genesis 18 and 19, where angels visiting Abraham and Lot are described as accepting human hospitality and even consuming earthly sustenance like food. Perhaps most striking is the account in Genesis 32, where an angel engages the patriarch Jacob in a physical wrestling match, going so far as to injure Jacob's hip, demonstrating that these celestial messengers were capable of interacting with humans on an equal, physical footing. Taken together, these biblical narratives present a fascinating portrait of angels that departs from the common conception of them as purely ethereal, disembodied spirits, instead imbuing them with a striking degree of human-like qualities and capabilities. This complicates our understanding of the angelic realm and its relationship to the mortal world in profound ways.

According to the biblical accounts, angels are celestial beings who occasionally take on human form in order to interact with and guide mortals. When such divine messengers appear before people, they often reveal their true angelic nature, shedding light on the profound spiritual realm beyond our earthly existence. If a person were to encounter one of these otherworldly entities and then attempt to embrace them, the angel's reaction would likely be one of understanding and compassion. After all, angels are deeply attuned to the emotional and physical needs of humanity, having been entrusted by the divine to watch over and care for God's children. They understand the innate human desire for physical connection and comfort, and would no doubt recognize the sincere, reverent intention behind such a gesture. Rather than recoiling or displaying discomfort, the angel would probably allow the hug to occur, recognizing it as a heartfelt expression of awe, gratitude, and the yearning to commune with the sacred. In that moment, the human would be granted a rare glimpse into the realm of the divine, experiencing firsthand the gentle, benevolent nature of these celestial beings who have been sent to provide guidance, protection, and spiritual sustenance to those dwelling in the mortal world. The angel's acceptance of the embrace would convey a profound sense of grace, reminding the person of the profound love and care that the heavenly host extend to humanity, even in our most vulnerable moments of need.

May the divine blessings of the Almighty envelop your life in a profound and transformative way, as if you are being gently embraced by a legion of celestial guardians like never before. Allow this newfound spiritual awareness to permeate your very being, granting you a more enlightened perspective on the mysteries of existence. Recognize that the divine presence of God is ever-present, a constant companion guiding your steps and uplifting your soul. Take solace in the knowledge that you are never truly alone, for there is always a watchful angel by your side, a benevolent protector shielding you from harm and illuminating your path forward. Let this unwavering celestial support fill your heart with a profound sense of peace, reassurance, and the unwavering certainty that you are divinely loved and cared for, no matter the challenges you may face. Open your eyes and your spirit to the wondrous, unseen forces that surround you, for in doing so, you will find yourself enveloped in the comforting embrace of the divine, your life forever transformed by this deep, abiding spiritual connection. Trust in the angels that walk beside you, for they are the manifestation of God's eternal love, ever-present guardians dedicated to your well-being and the fulfillment of your highest purpose.

God bless.